Wedded Bliss

grayscale coloring book

curated by
Tabz Jones

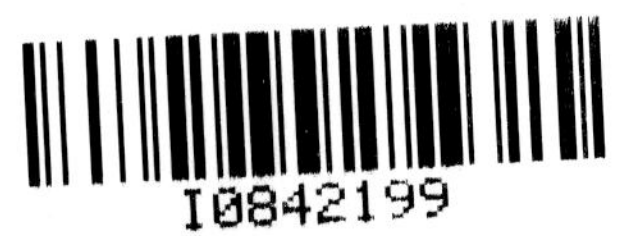

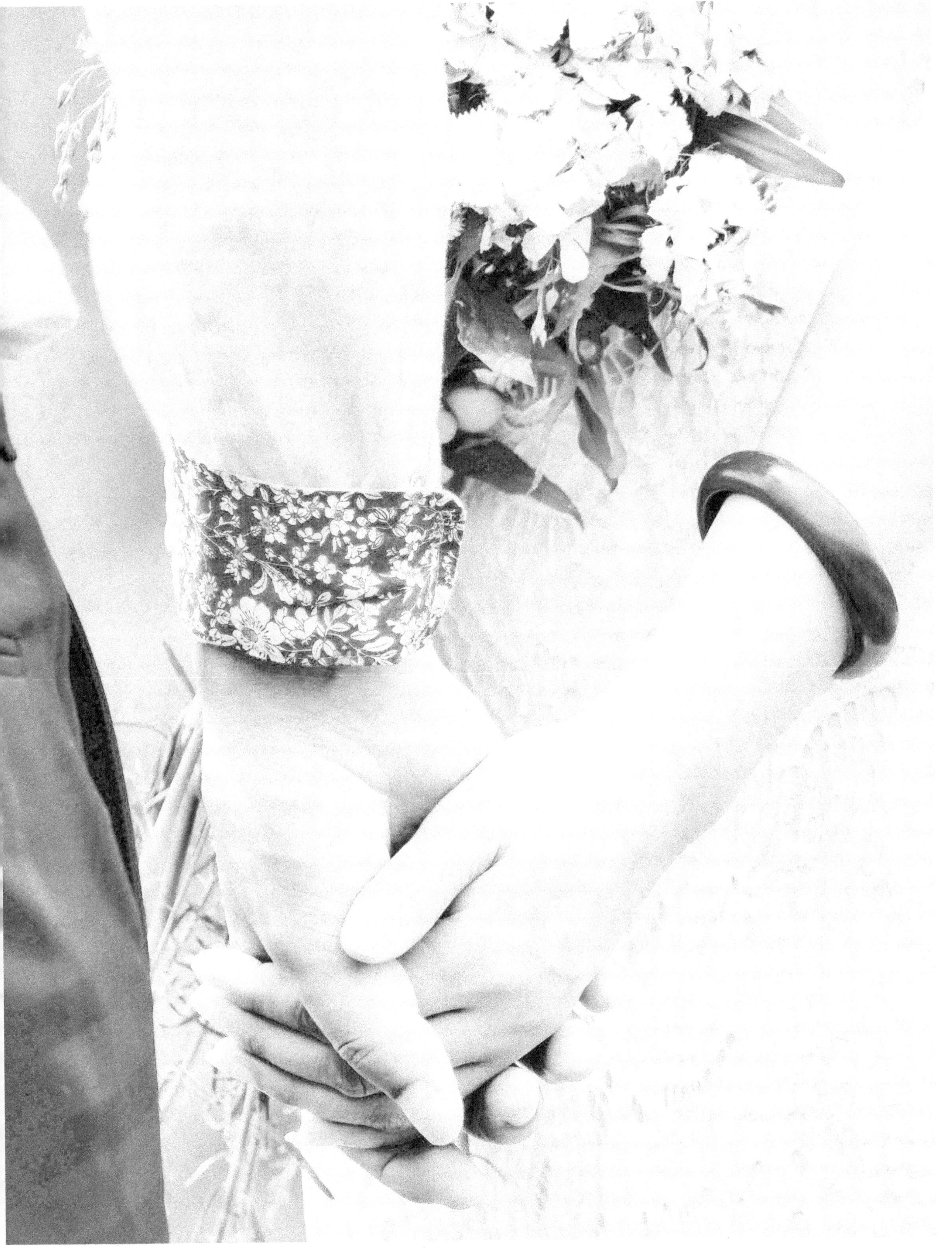

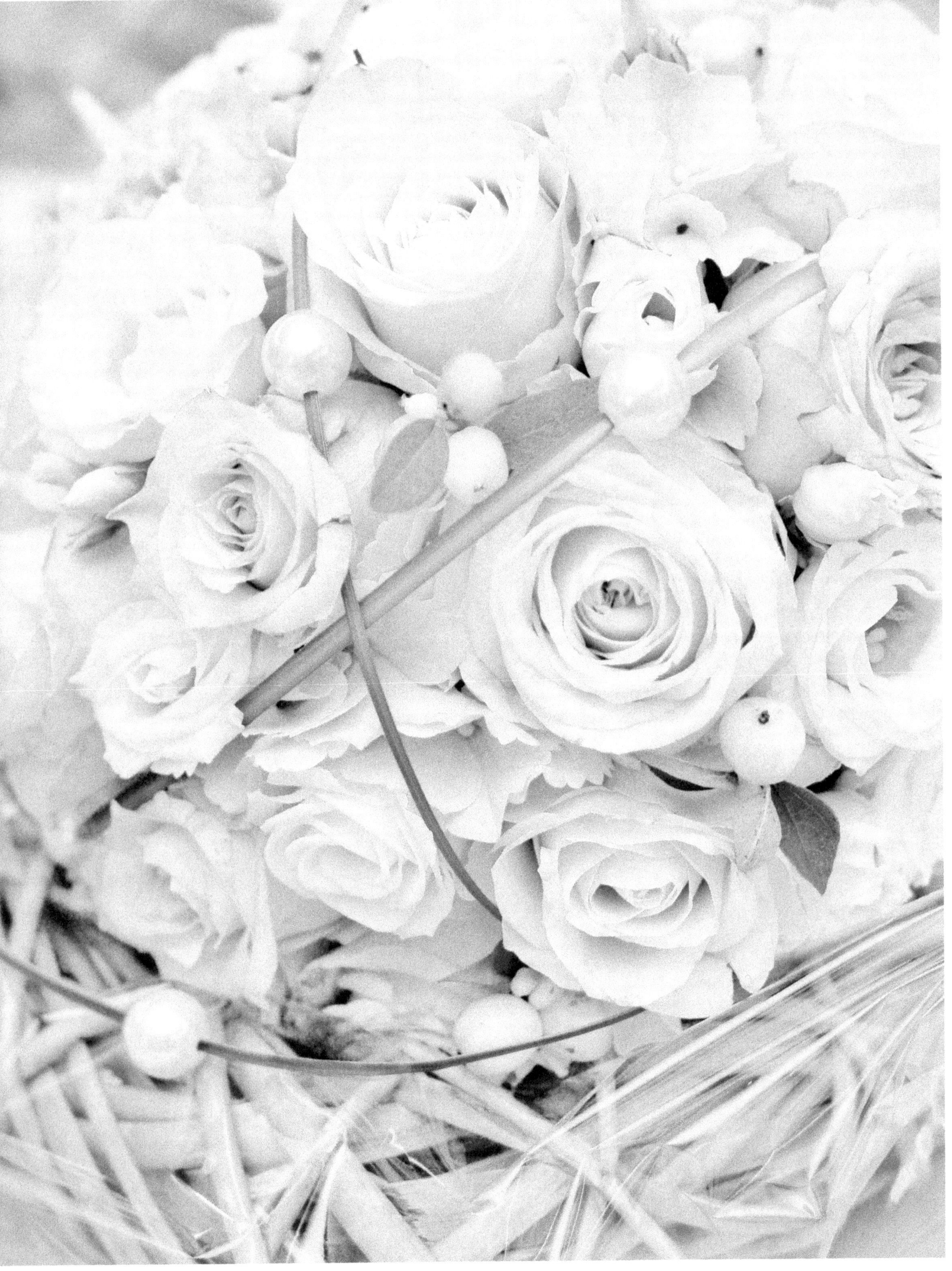

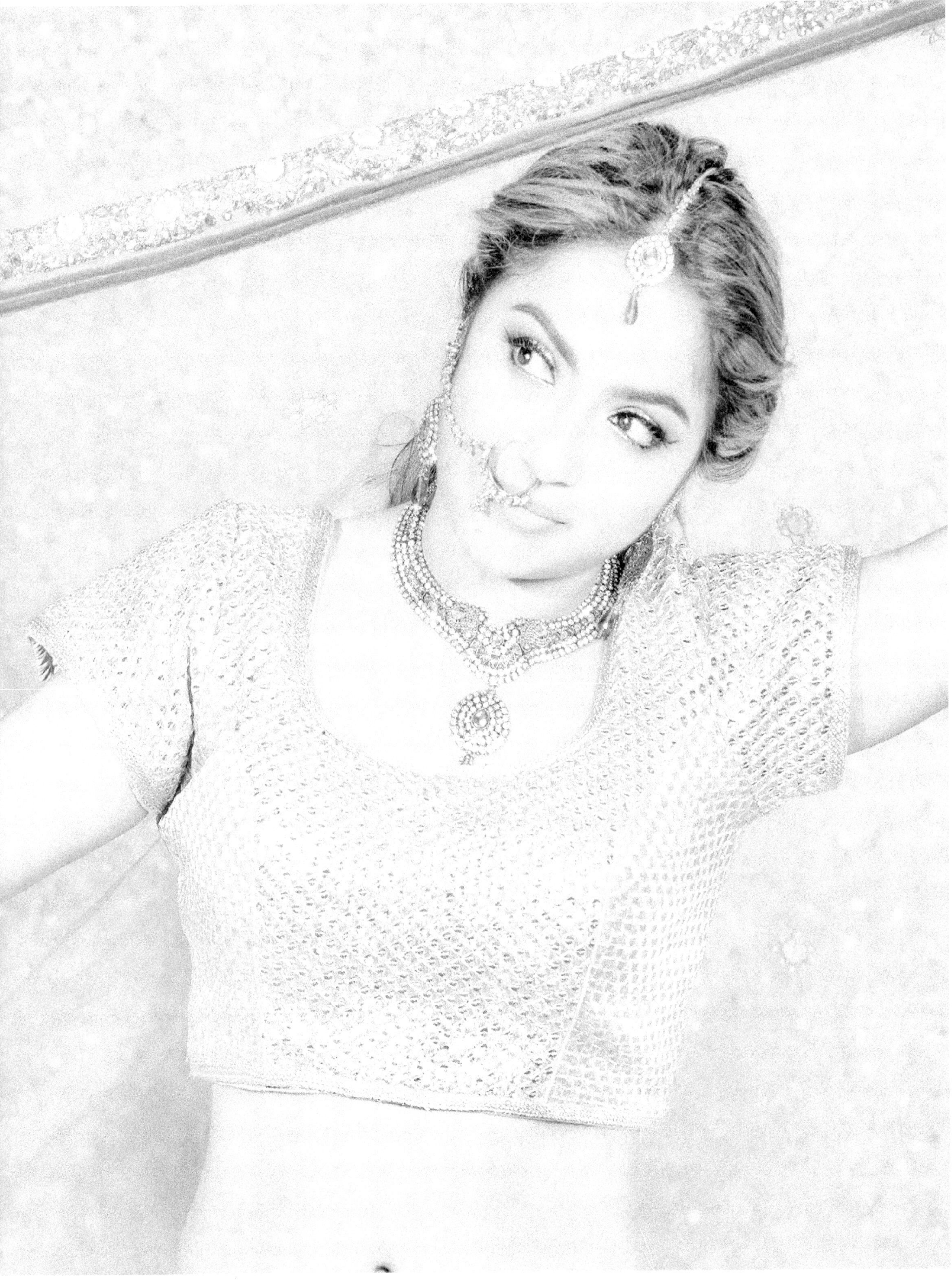

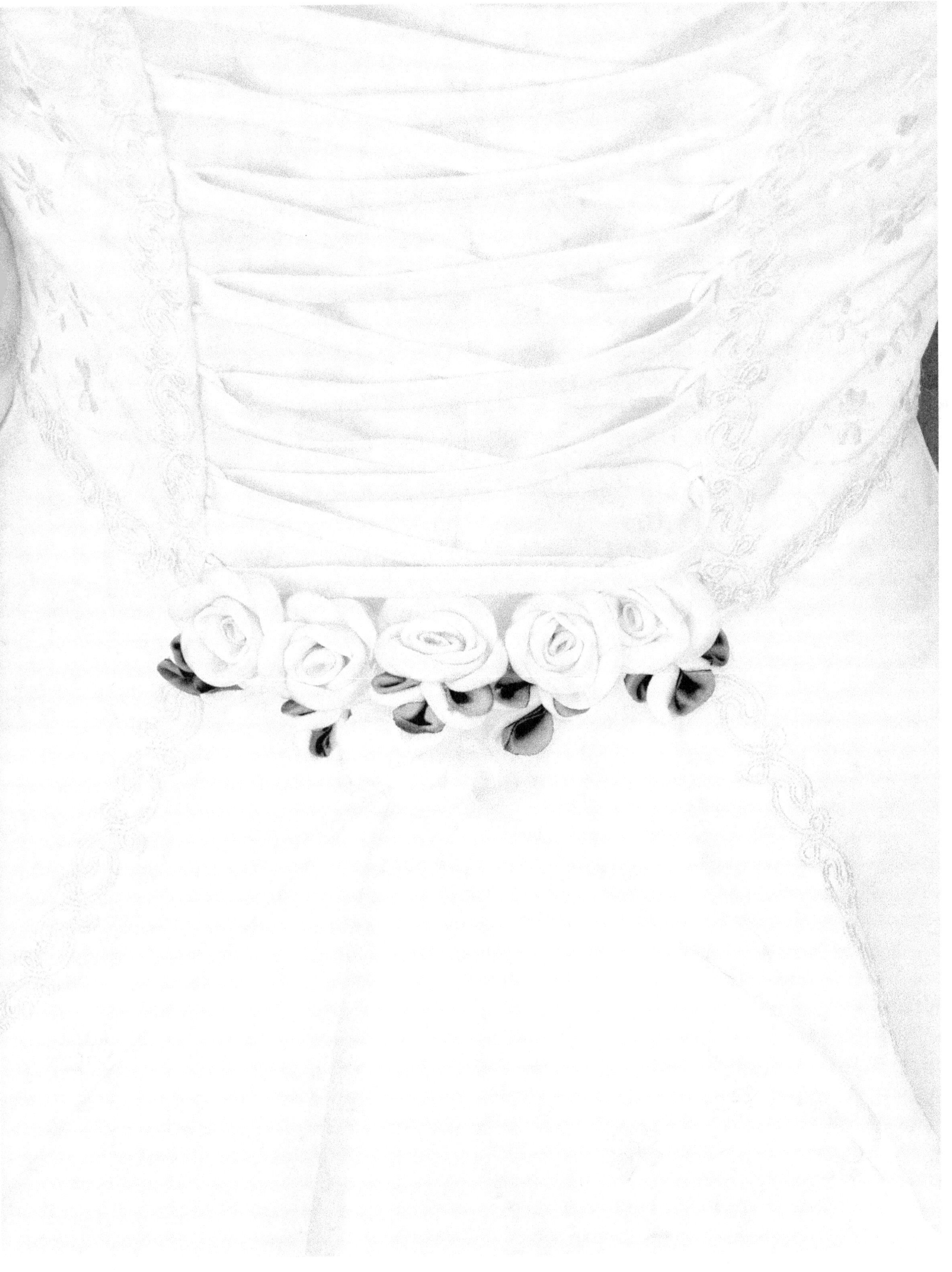

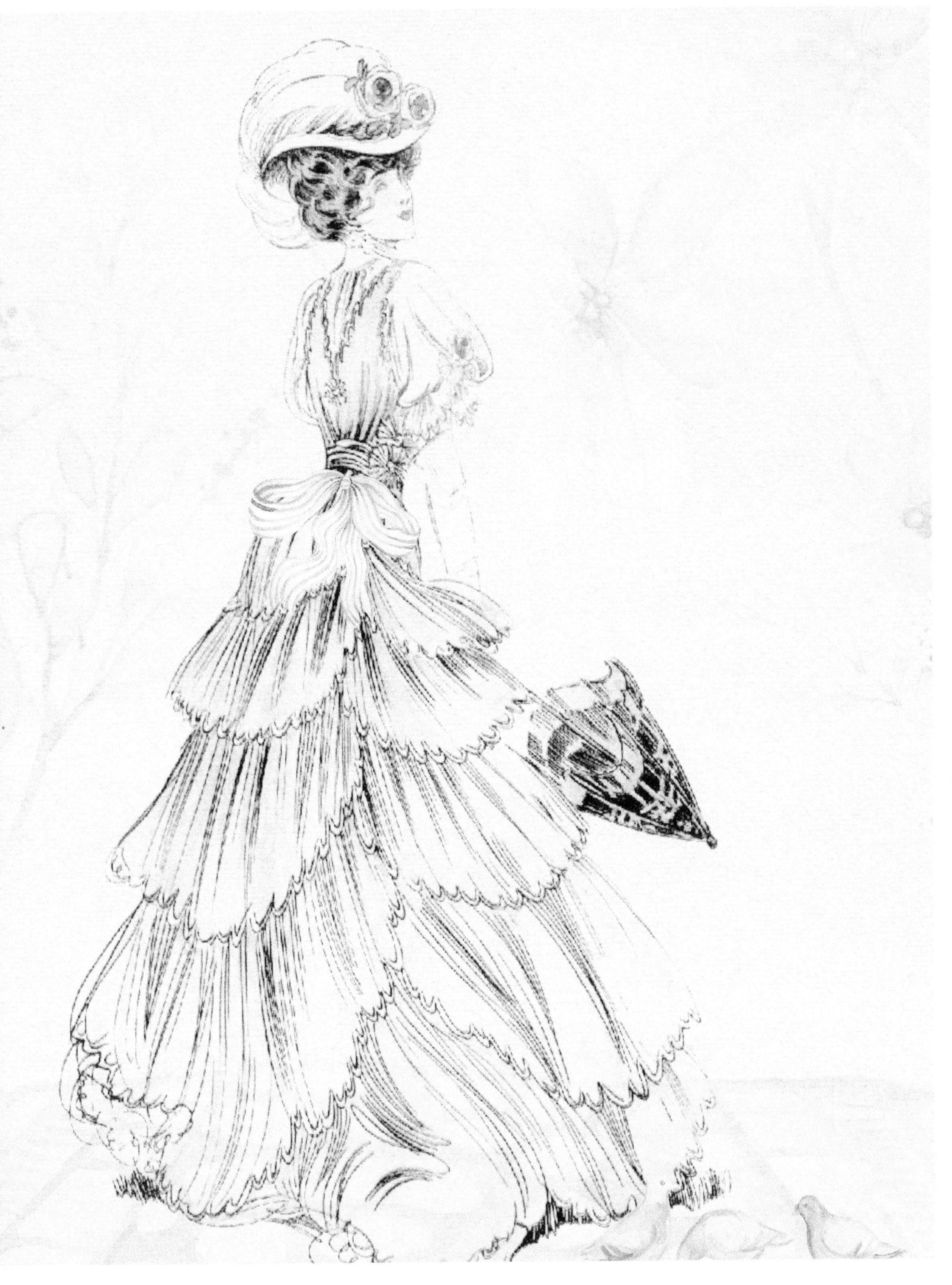

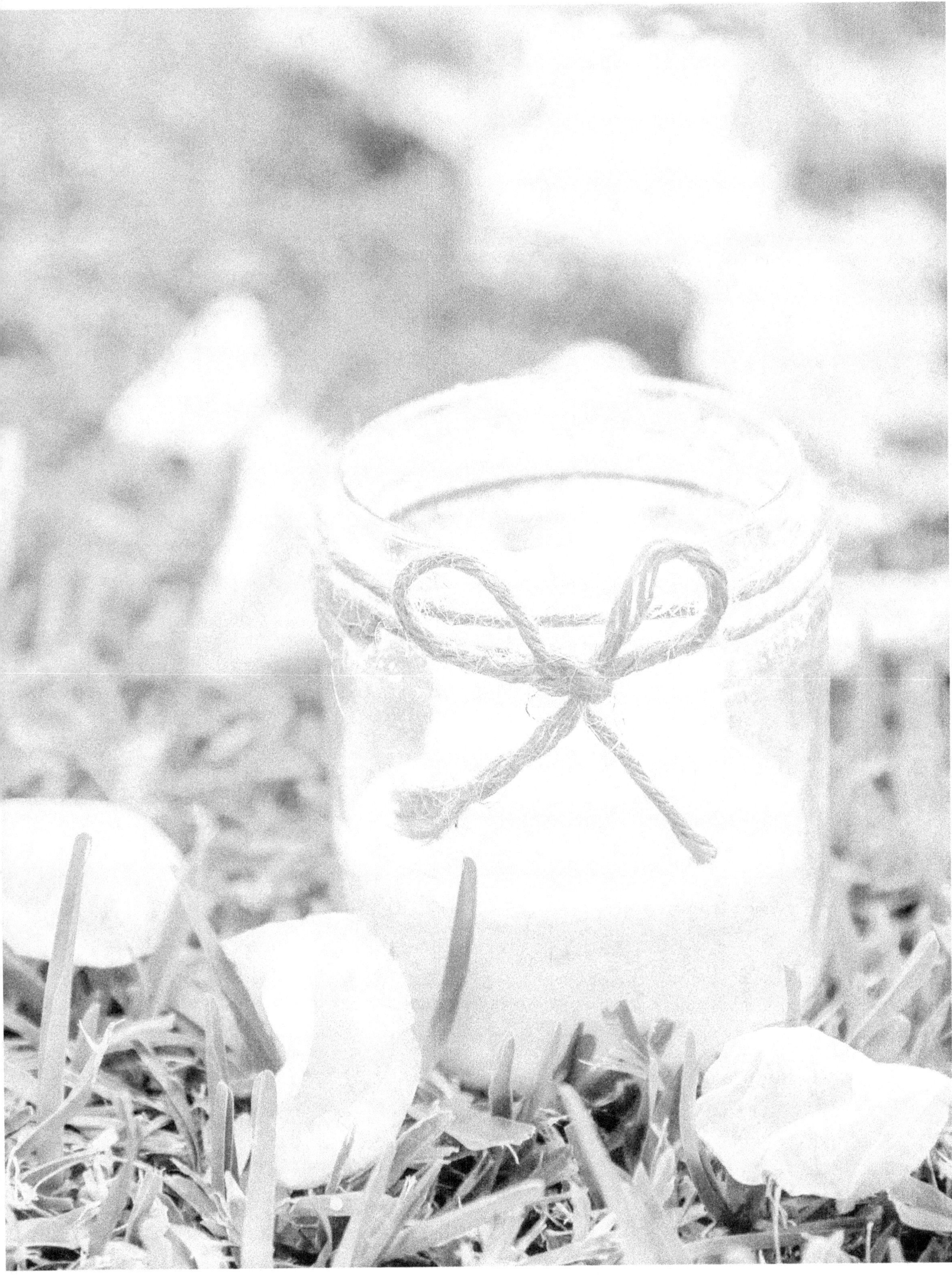

Wedding Day

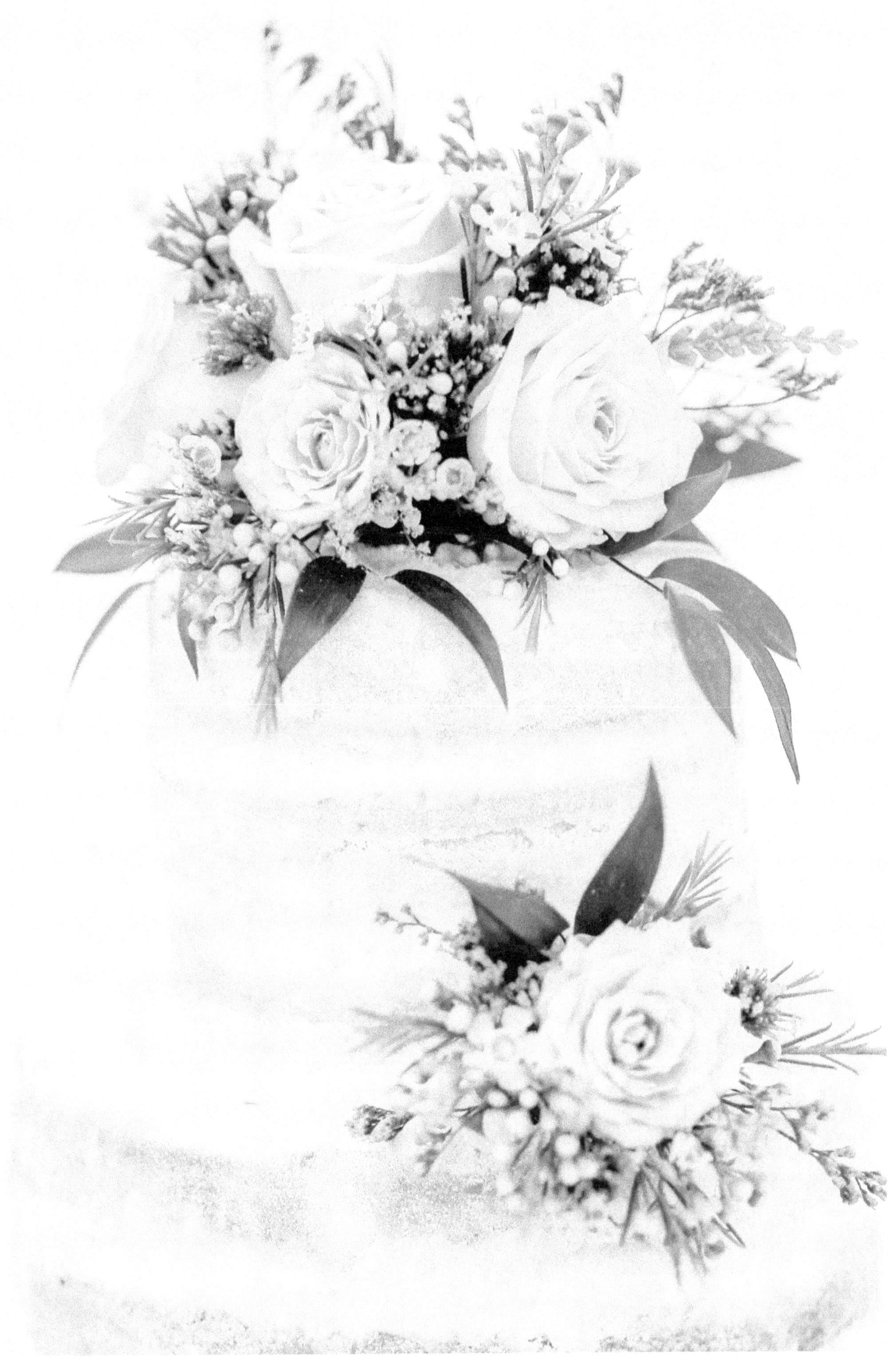

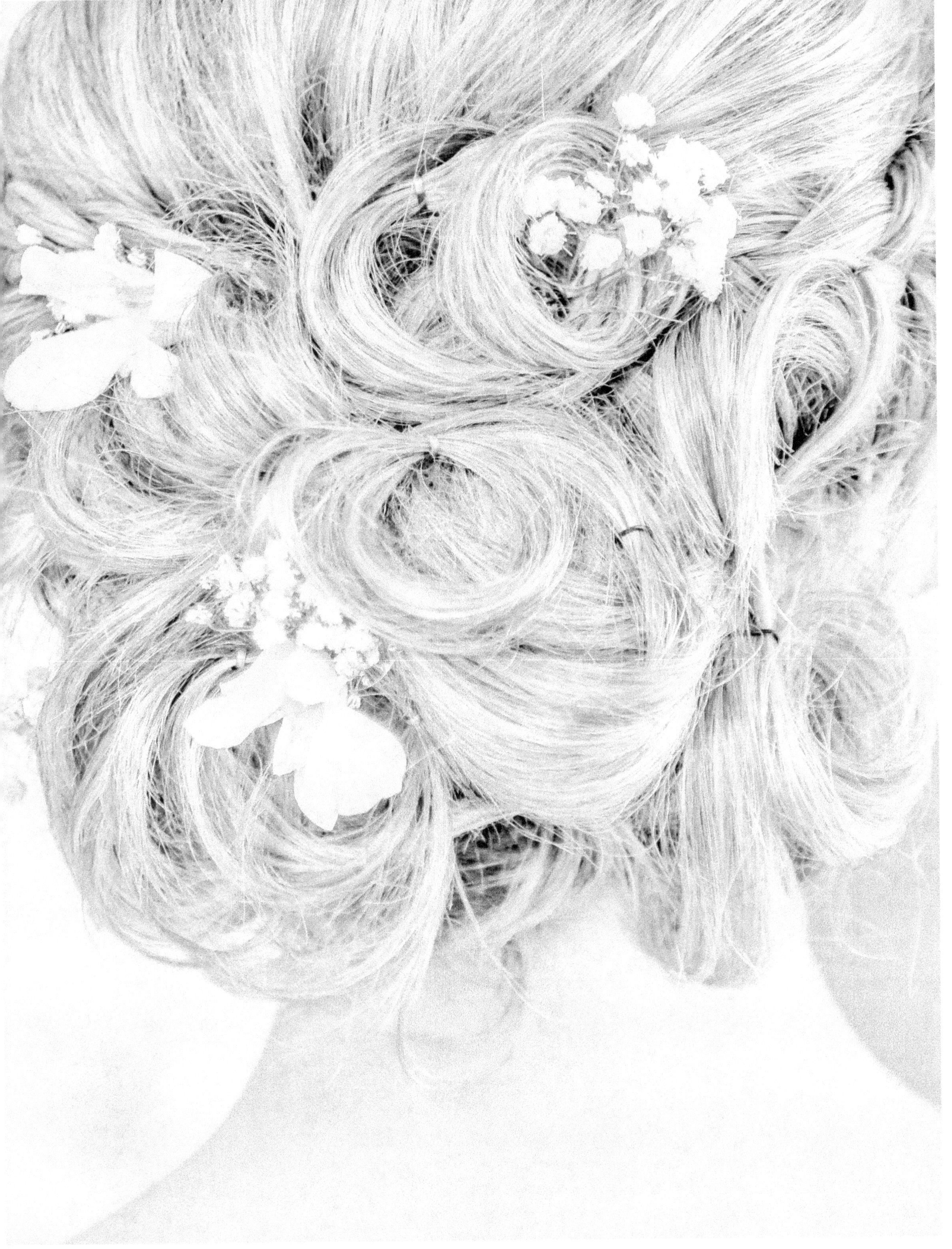

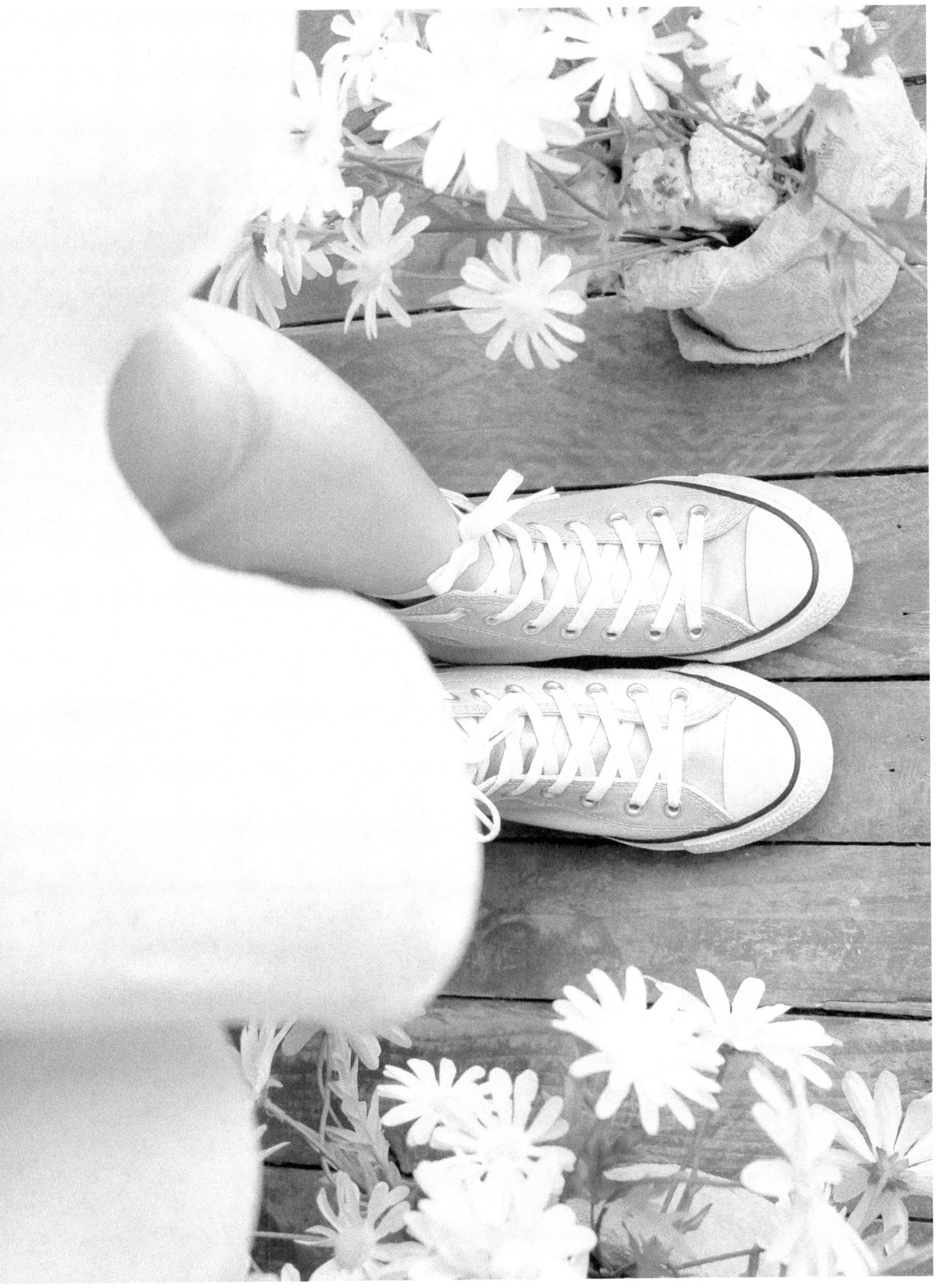

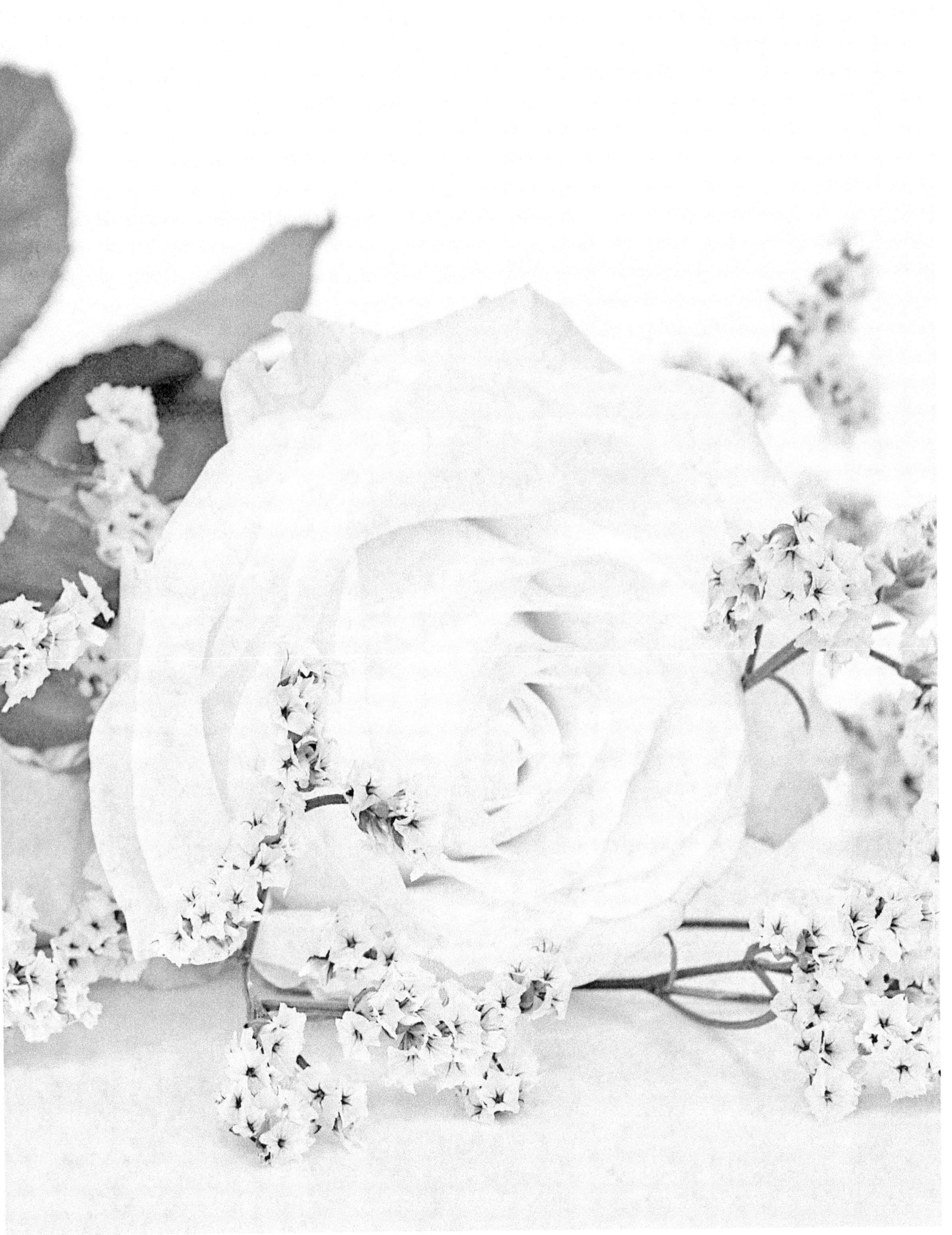

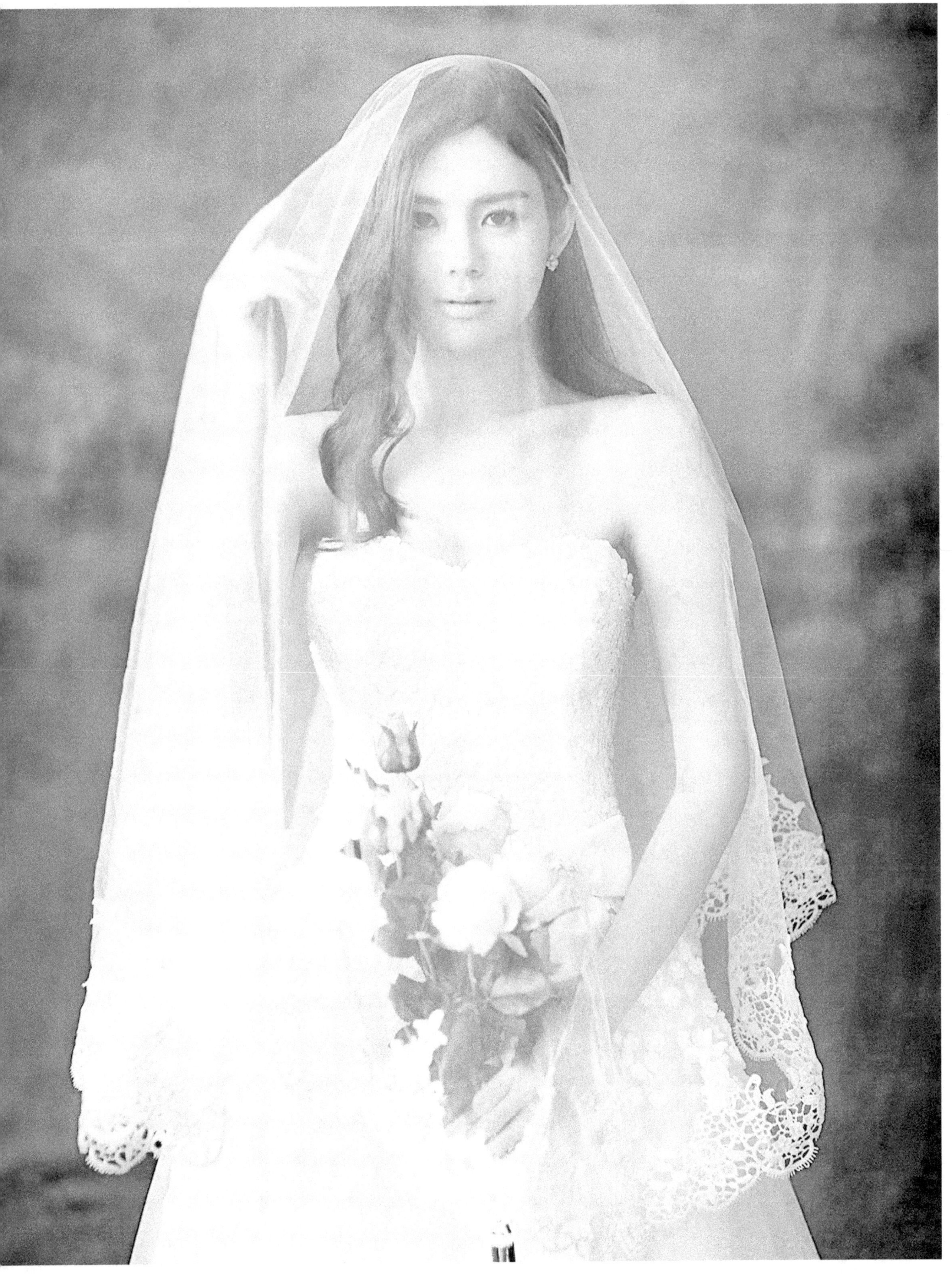

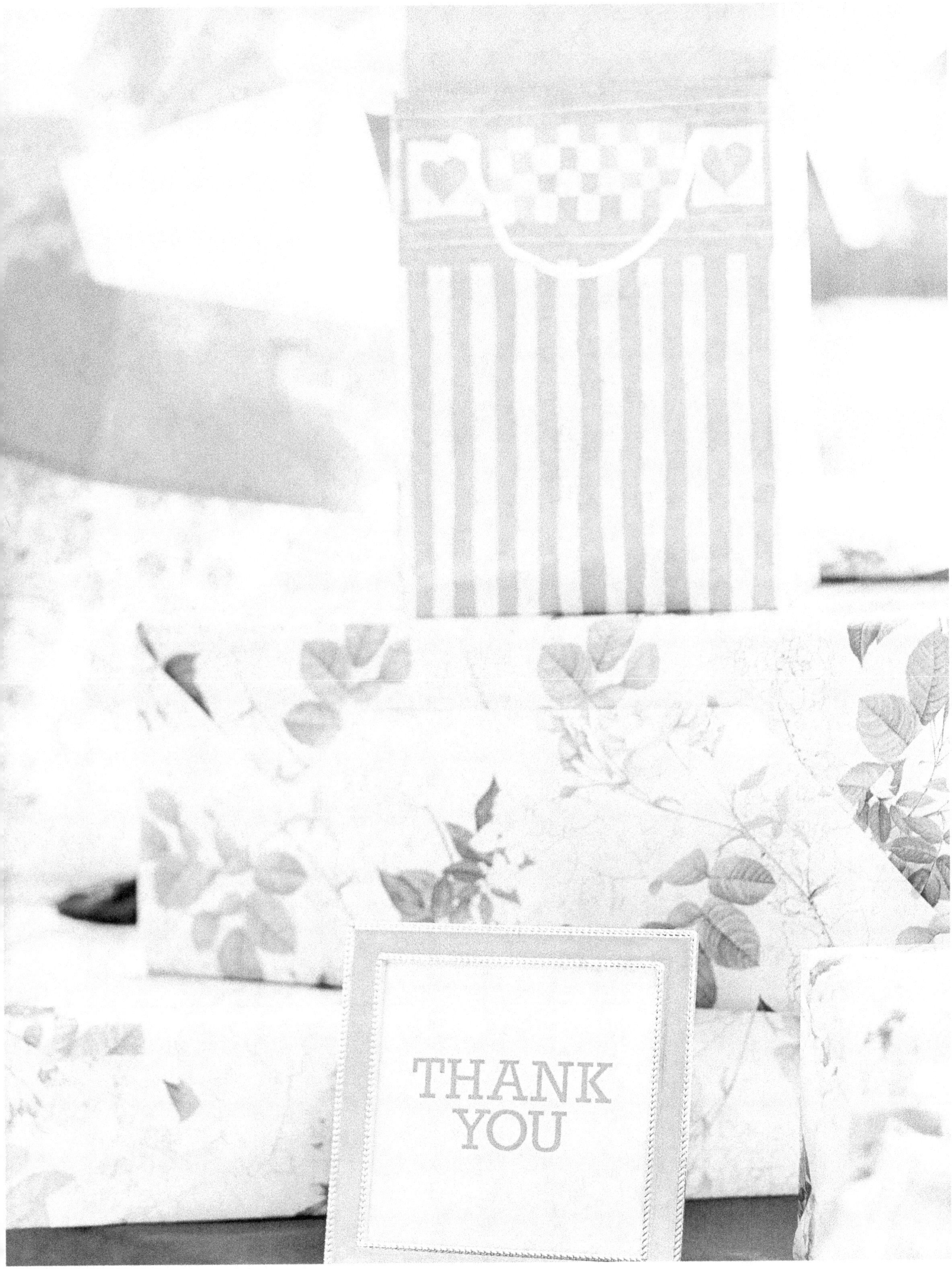

THANK
YOU

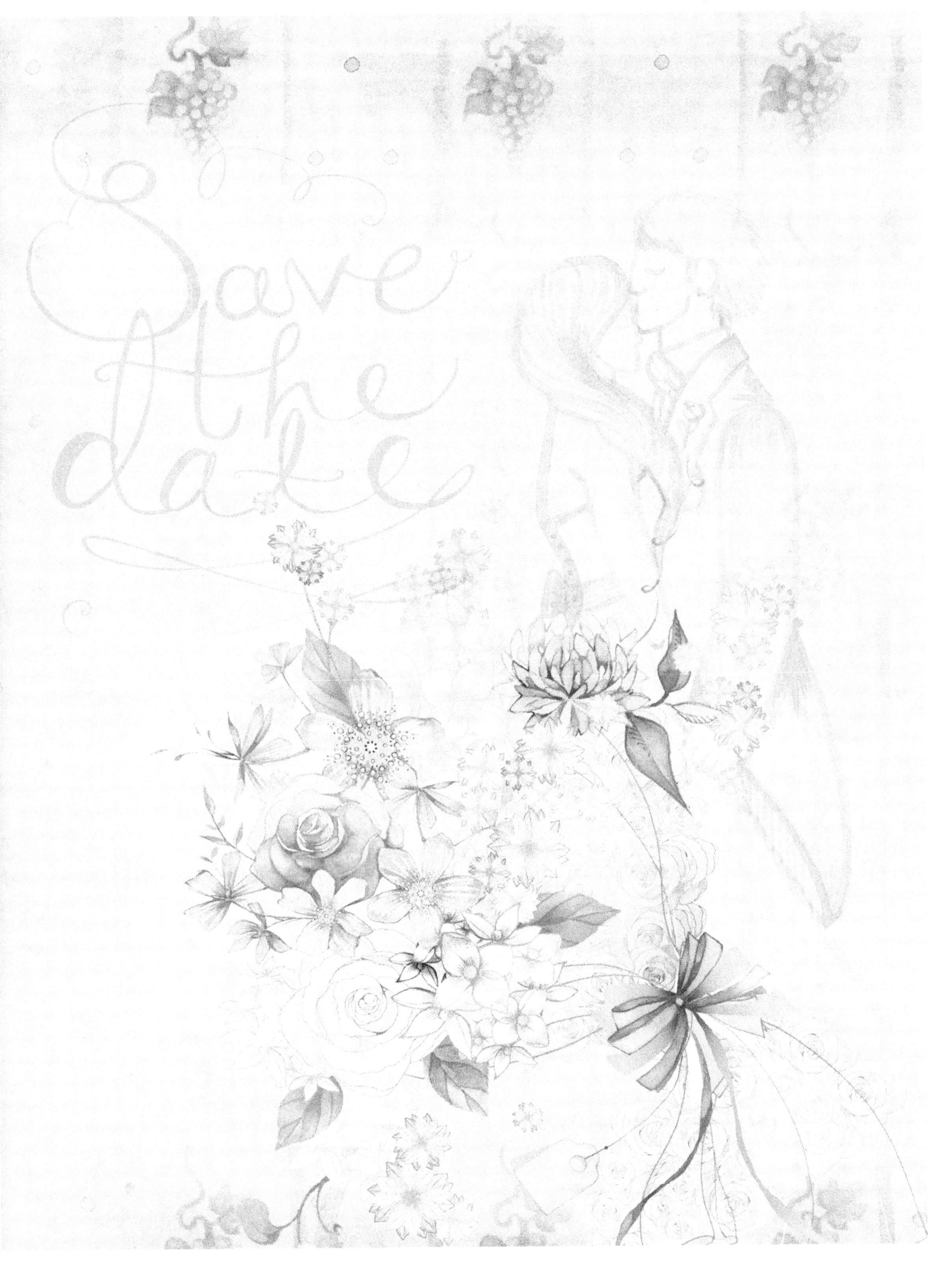
Save the date

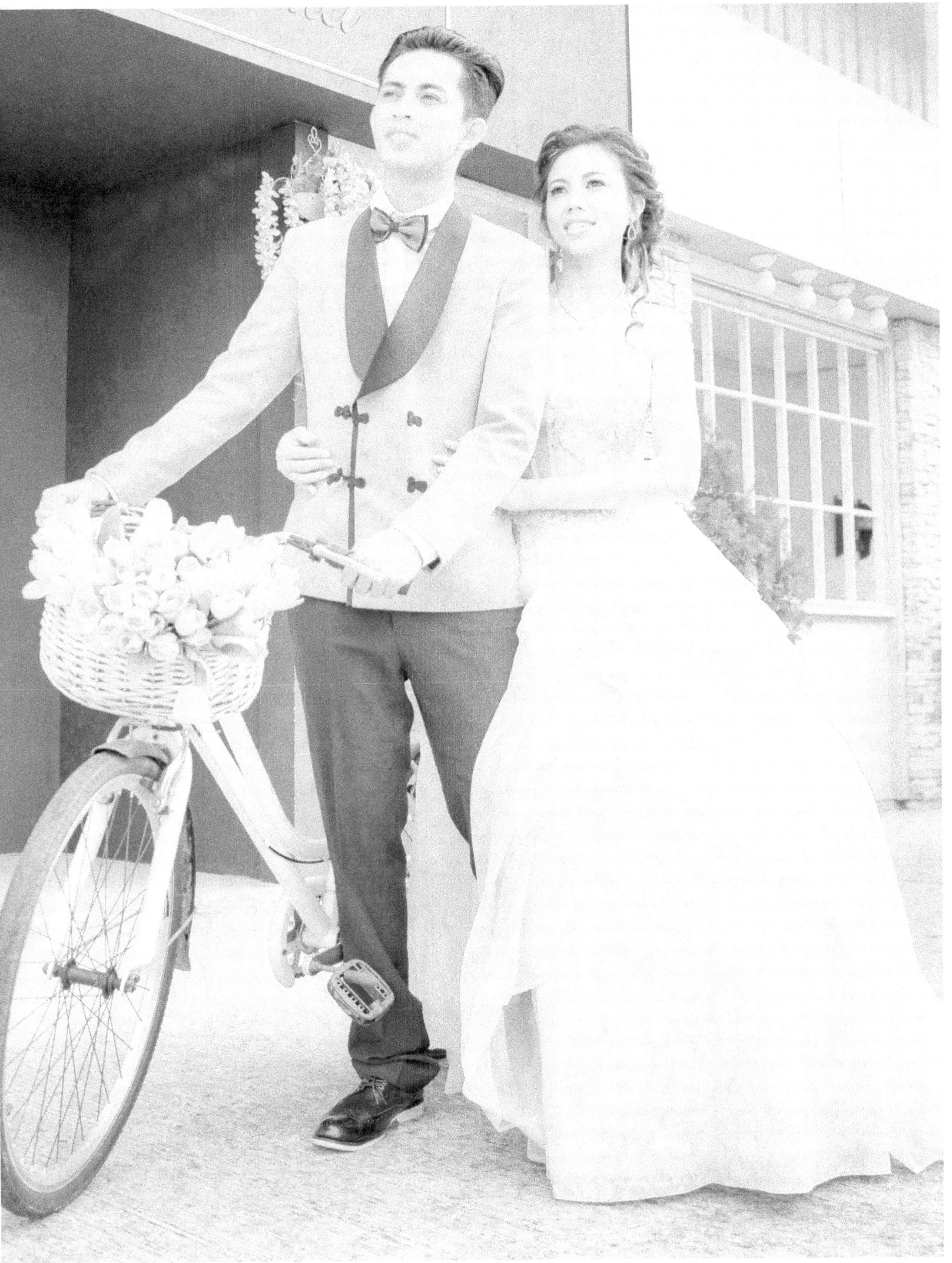

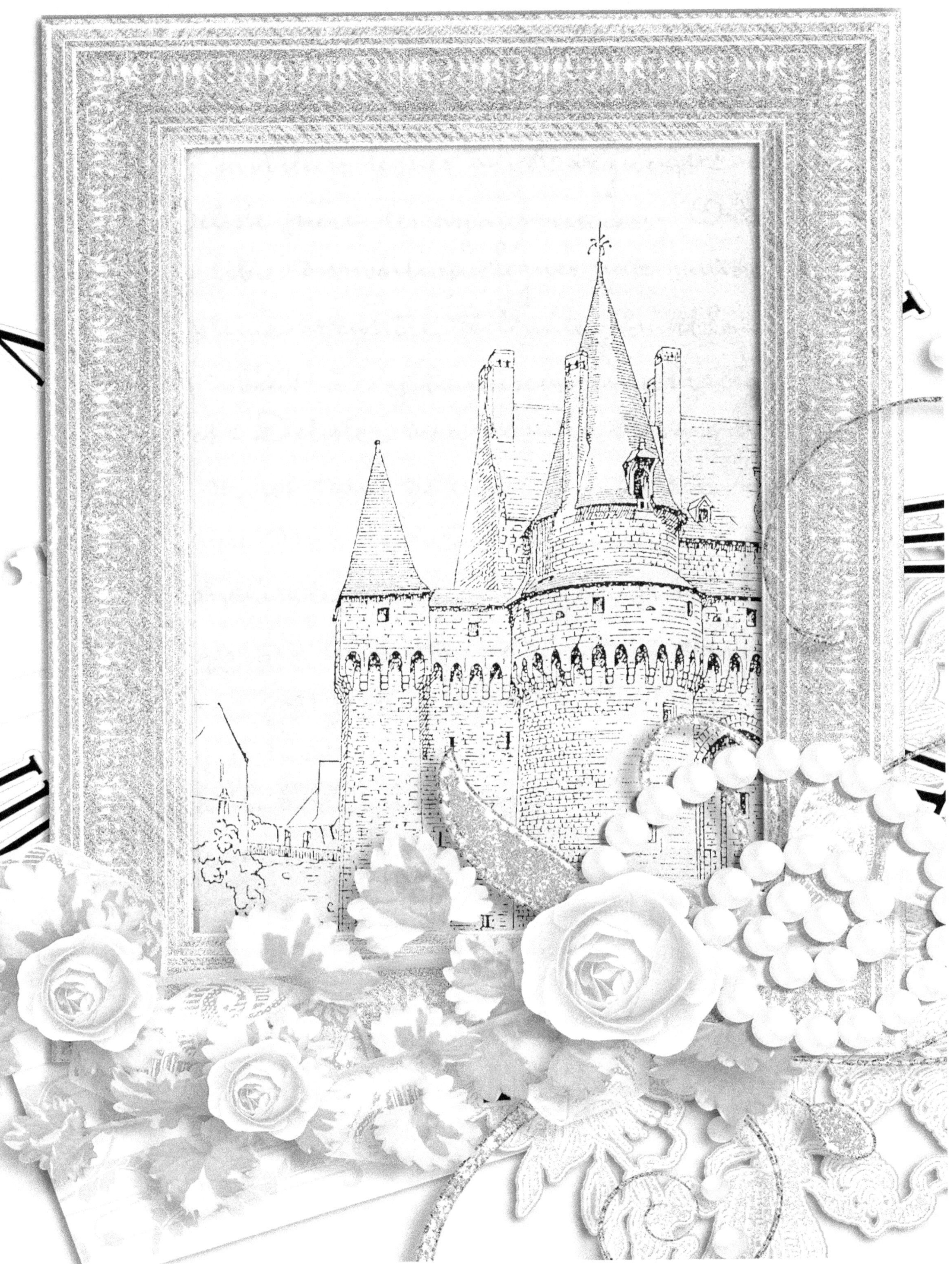

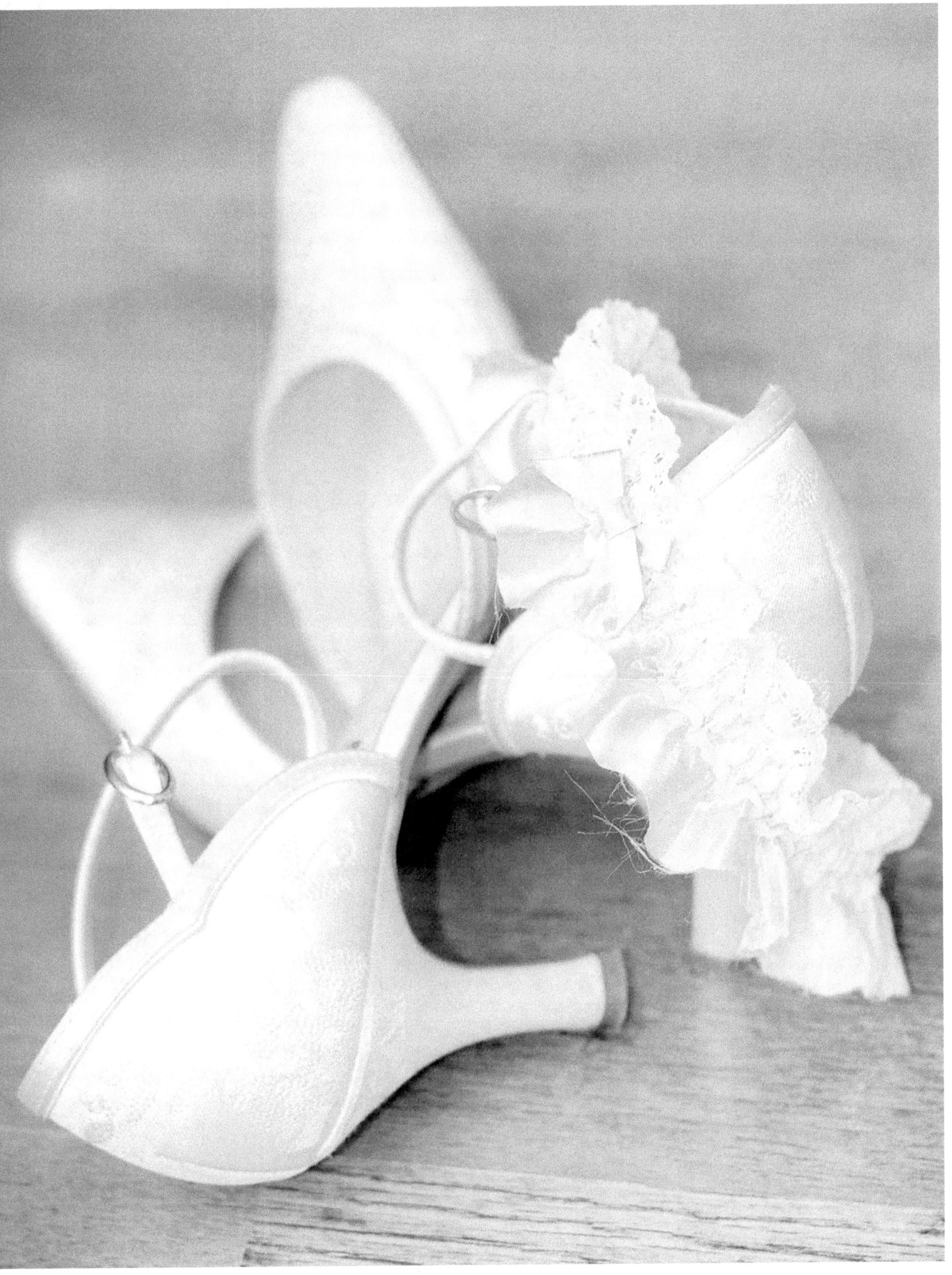

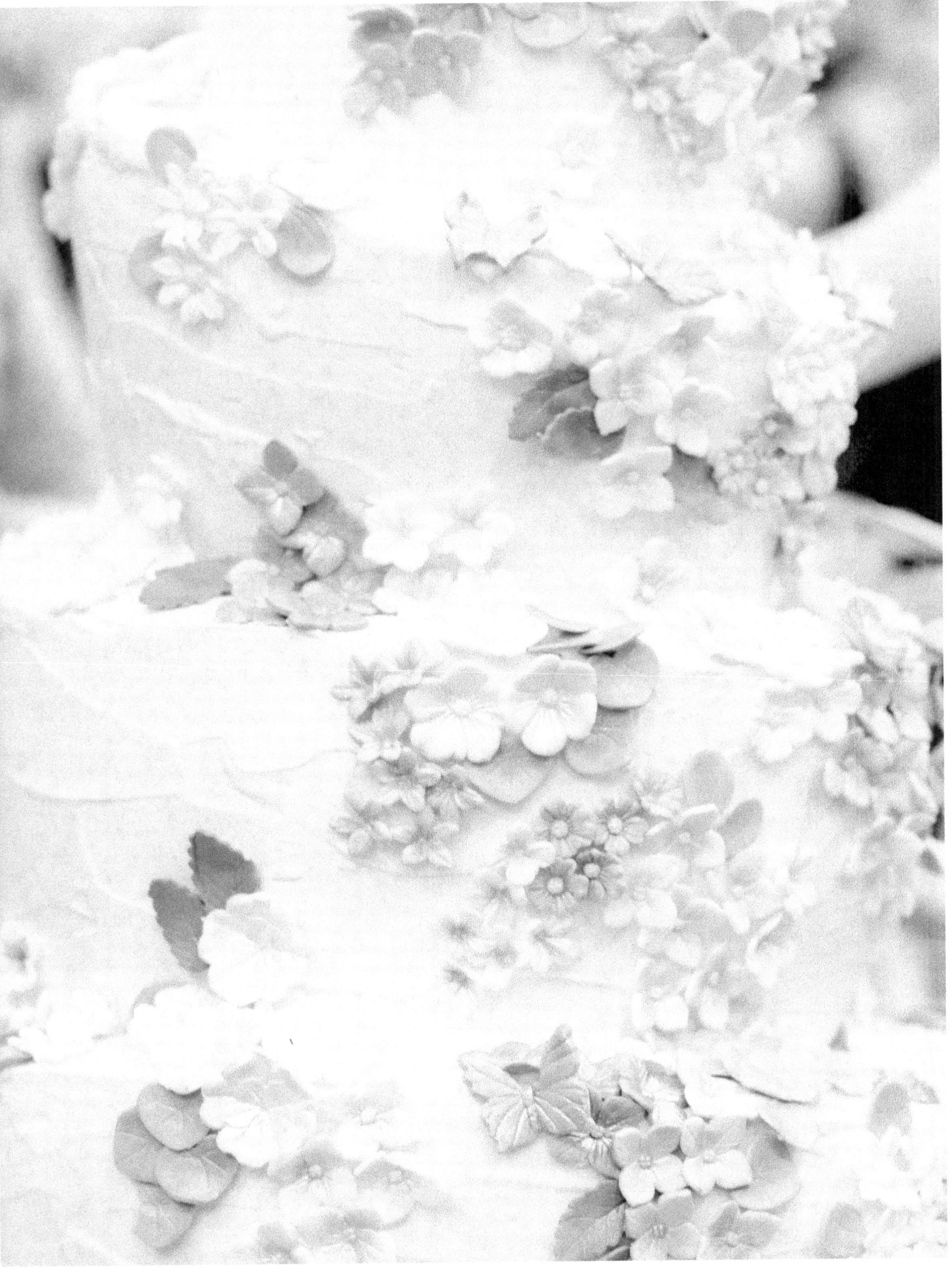

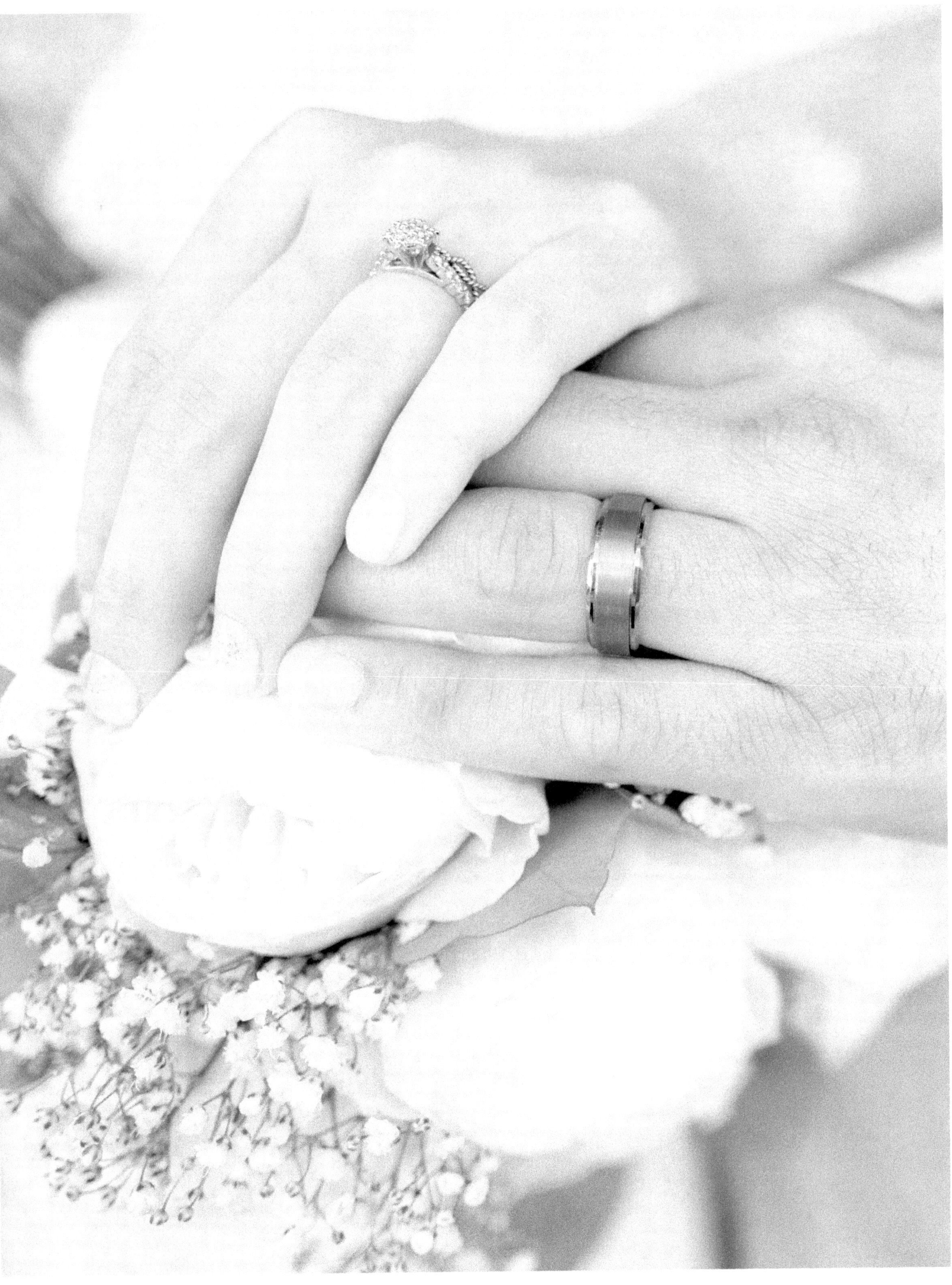

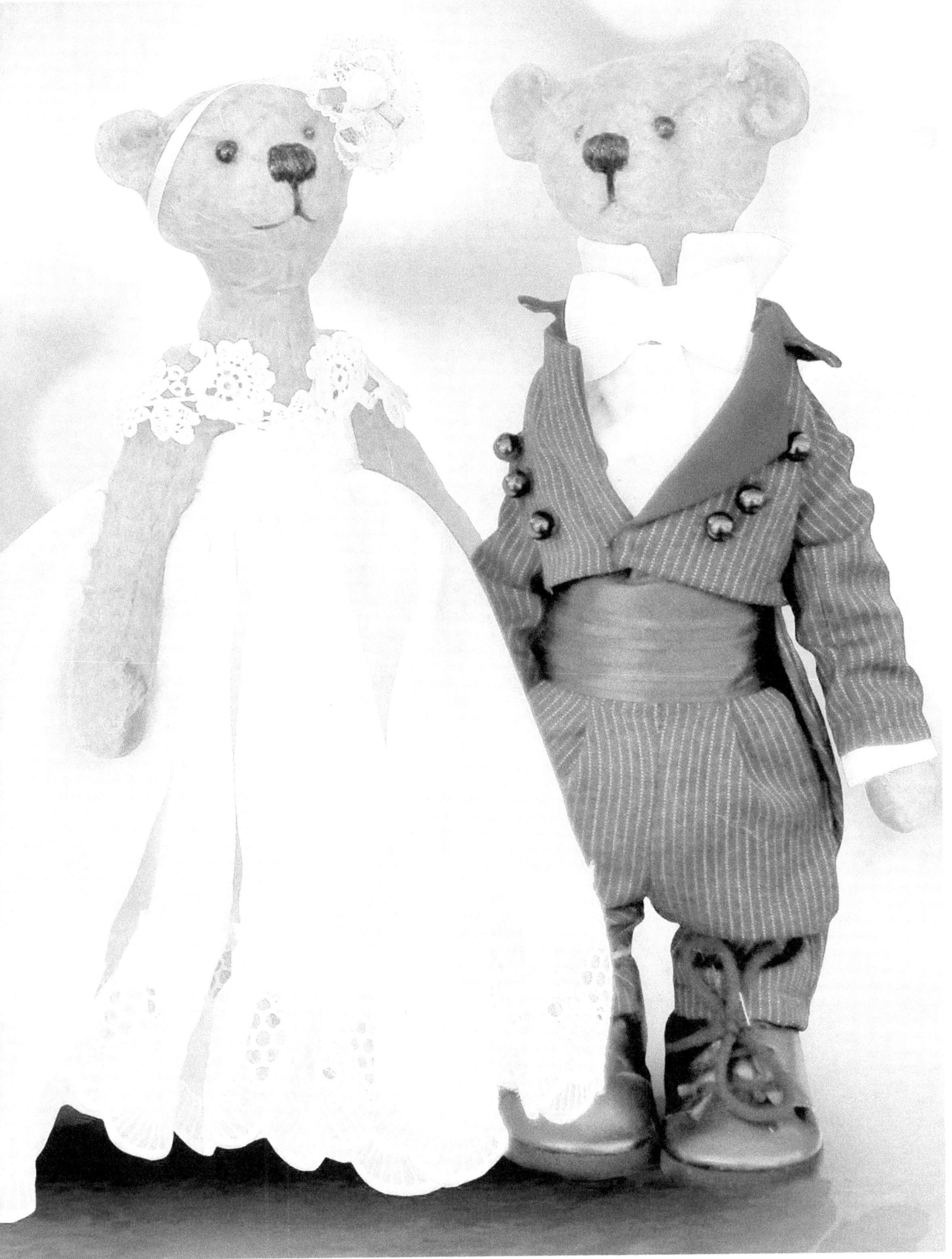

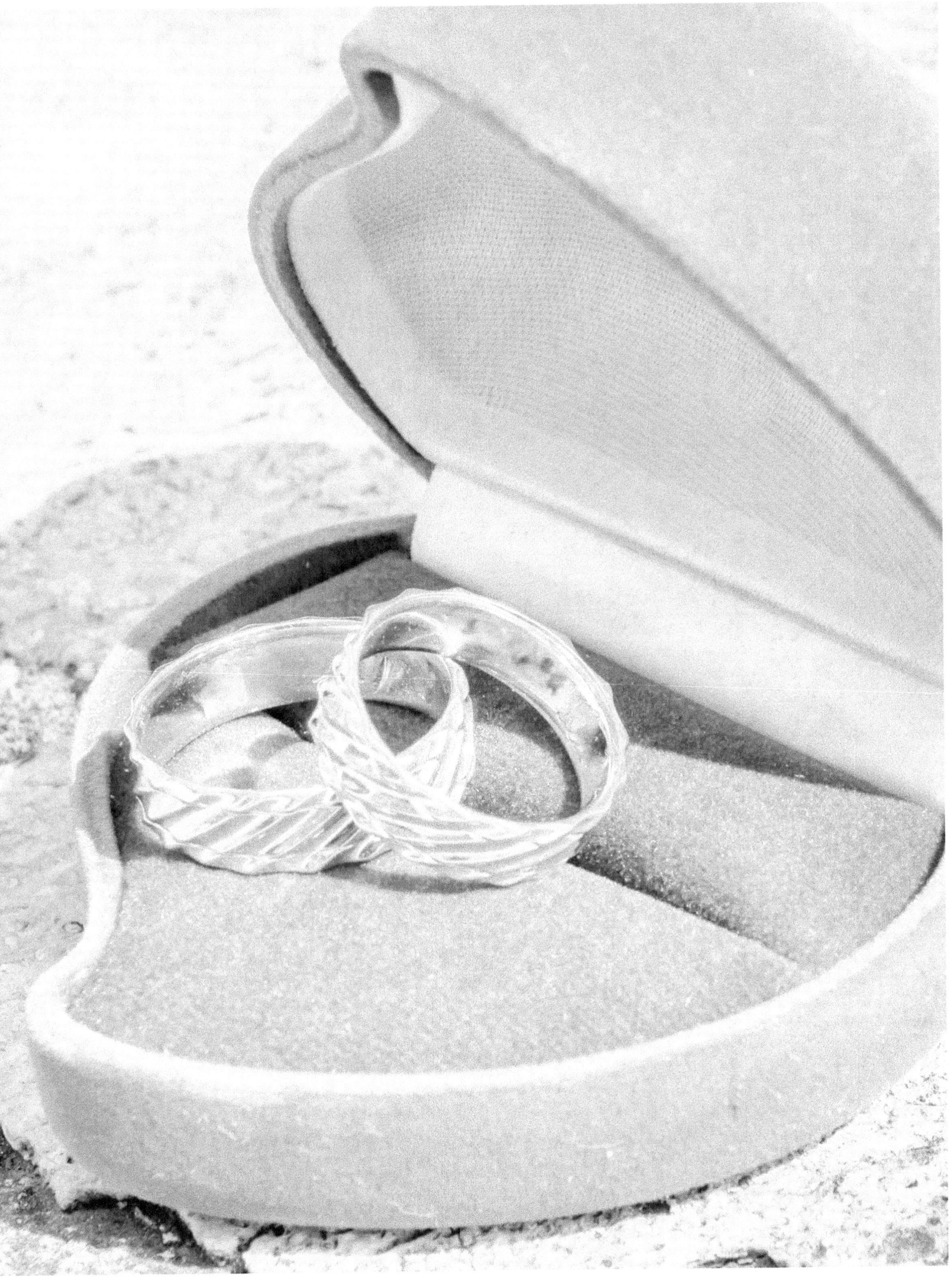